Entrepreneur Secrets

How to Build Wealth and Escape the Rat Race

Rick Markley

Table of Contents

Introduction

The word "entrepreneur" comes from the French verb "entreprendre" meaning "to do" or "to undertake." An entrepreneur is someone who "does", someone who acts. Generally, this means putting the time, energy, and money into starting up a business, and being willing to take the risks that come along with it. Whereas most people see problems, entrepreneurs see opportunities. Whereas most people complain about problems, entrepreneurs create solutions.

Small businesses are the lifeblood of the economy. Nearly two-thirds of all new jobs created in the past fifteen years have come from small businesses, and over half of these businesses are run from home!

About one out of ten people work for themselves or for a small company. We're all very fortunate to live in a world that encourages the creation and growth of new businesses. The process of opening your own company is relatively easy.

But who can be an entrepreneur?

Anyone can be an entrepreneur. You may be a twenty year old kid with no money in the bank with just a good idea, and you can still build a company from scratch. You don't have to be old to create a business: Google, Facebook, and Dell are all examples of companies that were started by students. You don't need lot of money, either: Microsoft, Nike, Domino's Pizza, Hewlett-Packard, and Eastman Kodak are all examples of companies that were started with ten thousand dollars or less. Don't think that setting up a business is an intimidating task that requires a lot of work, money, and special talent.

The question "Who can be an entrepreneur?" wasn't really a fair one, was it? If I asked, "Who can play golf?" and you answered "Anyone," you'd be technically right - just about anyone can pick up a club and hit a ball. But the real question should be, "Who can play golf well?" Just about anyone can start a company, but being a successful entrepreneur requires a particular type of person, a lot of hard work, and a good measure of luck.

1. Being an Entrepreneur

Many people think that today's entrepreneurs were always entrepreneurs, and that they were born with some "entrepreneur gene" that directed them into starting up companies from an early age. In reality, many of the most successful entrepreneurs were people who worked for large corporations for many years, gaining experience, saving money, testing ideas, and making business contacts before venturing off on their own. Just about every large corporation you see today was at one time nothing more than an idea in some entrepreneur's mind.

Entrepreneurial Myths

This brings us to one of the myths about entrepreneurialism. We'll look at a few of the common entrepreneurial myths throughout this section.

MYTH #1: You need money, special skills, or connections to be an entrepreneur.

REALITY: Anyone can be an entrepreneur; you don't need anything but the right frame of mind.

Why Would Someone Become an Entrepreneur?

- Ambition (frame, fortune, dreams)

- Freedom, individuality, non-conformity

- Frustration with corporate environment

- Necessity (can't get a corporate job)

- Passion (can be a part-time passion)

- Fear (worried that you won't be successfully any other way)

- Charity (believe it's the best way to help society)

- DNA (it's in your blood)

- Stupidity (you harbor misconceptions about entrepreneurship)

- Because you can

MYTH #2: *Entrepreneurs are born with a gene that compels them to start businesses when they're young.*

REALITY: *Many entrepreneurs discover their calling only after years of going the "corporate route."*

Most people think that a "cost" is something measured in dollars, but that's not the case. An opportunity cost is what you sacrifice in order to do something. For example, if you have a choice of going to the movies with your friends Friday night or working on a business plan that's due Monday, the cost of staying home to work on the business plan is the lost enjoyment of hanging out with your friends.

Every decision carries opportunity costs, and the decision to set up and run a business can come with seemingly endless ones. Real success is about finding and maintaining a healthy balance in life, and that means knowing when the opportunity costs for doing one thing and not another are too high. It means being able to prioritize.

Having a business can mean having something that knows no boundaries; it can intrude on every aspect of your life if you let it. Something you should do if you're going to set up and run a business while keeping up with your family and maintaining some kind of social life is put up "fences" around your non-business life.

Fences are borders. They're a way to partition off things so that your customers' calls don't spill over into your wedding day. You can create one fence by setting up a business phone number and keeping business hours. You might have a voice mail on your business phone that instructs people how to reach you in the event of an emergency, but otherwise you'll be erecting a barrier between your customers and your private life.

Whether the benefits of being an entrepreneur outweigh the drawbacks is something only you can decide, but the important thing to remember is that most entrepreneurs work harder, make less, enjoy less freedom, and have more stress than the person who gets a job at a big company. Don't harbor any glamorous illusions of what being a business owner is like. If you know what you're getting yourself into, you'll be better prepared for challenges when they arise.

MYTH #3: Owning a business is glamorous.

REALITY: Owning a business is hard work, long hours, lots of stress, and a ton of struggle.

MYTH #4: Being successful means taking big risks.

REALITY: Success is about defense as well as offense; it's about minimizing risk, not just maximizing opportunity.

This is one of the most common myths about starting a business. Being a successful entrepreneur isn't about taking risks; it's about avoiding or minimizing them without reducing the opportunity.

There's no way to eliminate risk entirely, but the more risks you can eliminate, the more you're able to focus on achieving your goals. Planning helps you identify and sidestep many of the risks that other, less prepared businesspeople exhaust themselves wrestling with.

2. The Main Rules of Business Success

Optimism

Optimism is a great characteristic of many business people. Most entrepreneurs have an abundance of optimism and young people in particular seem to have plenty of it.

Optimism is a fuel. It can propel you through obstacles that would stop the average person. When the average person is slumped over with his head in his hands, wondering why he can't get anyone to see the genius of his product and write him a check, the optimist will think past the moment, envisioning the day when his product is in every household and he's become a rock star of the business world. That ability to think positively, what less optimistic people might call "the ability to convincingly and repeatedly delude oneself into persevering against all odds", is perhaps the entrepreneur's greatest asset, though you'll never find it on a balance sheet.

Optimism is a double-edged sword. Optimism can be fuel, but it can also act like blinders. Optimists have a knack for glossing over risks and making forecasts and plans that are wildly unrealistic.

If you make statements like "there are six billion people on Earth; I expect to sell my product to only 10 percent of them, meaning that I will sell 600 million units," you will be treated as a fool. (Making the "the-potential-market-is-so-large-that-I-only-need-a-small-percentage-of-it-to-succeed" argument is a very common mistake that entrepreneurs make.)

The best way to avoid the killing end of the optimism sword is this: get into the habit of under-promising and over-delivering. Deliver more than you've promised, even if it means setting the bar for your business low at first.

The reason that others will judge you harshly is because unchecked optimism can appear to be a character flaw. If there's something wrong with your character - you're careless or prone to not considering risks - it can be a very difficult thing to change. If your optimism continually gets the better of you, leading you to paint overly rosy pictures of what you and your business can deliver, you risk losing credibility with people you need to have on your side.

Don't let your optimism, a great strength for an entrepreneur, run rampant. Always be able to highlight risks to your scenarios and ideas, and explain how you intend to circumvent or overcome these risks.

On the opposite end of the weakness spectrum from character-based weaknesses are skill-based ones. Skill-based weaknesses are judged less harshly because they are easier to overcome. That is why if an interviewer ever asks you for a strength and weakness give them a character-based strength and a skill-based weakness.

What does that mean? It means that the strengths you identify are things rooted in your character: honesty, dependability, loyalty, intelligence, creativity, and so on. On the other hand, when you discuss a weakness, make sure it's a skill-based one: you're not good at typing or have problems using Excel, for example. You tell an interviewer a skill that you're weak at, and then explain what you're doing to address that weakness: "I know this position requires that I be proficient in Excel, and my weakness is that I don't have very much experience at using that kind of program. I've signed up for an online course in using Excel, though, and I'm a very fast learner."

Remember, the reason you highlight character-based strengths and skill-based weaknesses is that you can erase any skill-based weakness fairly easily. If you have a character-based weakness, that's a hard thing to fix.

Similarly, if you don't have a credit history, you can create one. If you can't get a loan from a bank, you can find other sources of capital. In comparison, if you have a character flaw - if you let your optimism impair your judgment and lead you to ignore risks and create unrealistic plans - that's a deep-rooted problem.

Impatience

Impatience is another double-edged sword. Impatience can lead to unnecessary action and immediate change. These can be good things, but you need to understand the walls you're charging into are going to give way sooner or later. Energy, enthusiasm, and demand for change can remove many obstacles in an entrepreneur's way, but some things require a more subtle approach. Sometimes, the world's not going to move at the pace you want it to, but you can't let that stop you.

Another negative example of impatience is that it can take you off your focus if the results you expected aren't materializing. You and your friends may start a business designing web sites for local restaurants. You figure you can sign a few customers pretty quickly and be making a couple thousand dollars a month by the end of your third month of operations.

Five months in, though, you find that a lot of restaurants just don't have the money to pay you to make a web site. Your partners start drifting, spending less time on the business. Pretty soon, your interests start to drift too, and the business goes into limbo.

There's a balance between being slow, cautious, contemplative, being aggressive, fast, and action-oriented. The more you can maintain that balance, the greater your likelihood of success. Set realistic goals, and anticipate slow starts. Plan for the "bad case"; then, if something good does happen, it's more of a motivator. Aiming low and beating expectations - at least when you're starting out - can be a better path than aiming really high and continually undershooting.

Reality

Potential entrepreneurs should ask themselves why they are taking the start-up path. Are you doing it for money, for freedom, or for glamour? Are you going to be a part-time or a full-time entrepreneur? Do you have romanticized ideas of what being an entrepreneur means and are you prepared for the trade-offs, sacrifices, and possible setbacks?

If you have realistic expectations of yourself, your partners, and your business idea, it's far less likely you'll be disappointed with your results. A big reason many entrepreneurs give up on a business is that they are disappointed that their too lofty expectations weren't met in a short period of time. Success takes time. The chance of you coming up with the next big thing in business and striking it rich overnight is about the same as winning the lottery, maybe less.

Know what you're getting yourself into, set realistic expectations, and be persistent. Of course, if you don't have a good business to begin with, all the character and skill-based strengths in the world won't matter. Knowing if you've got an idea that could be a successful business is the topic of the next chapter.

3: Deciding Which Business to Go Into

There are eight key steps for deciding which business to go into:

1. Identify a problem.

2. Ask, "Would the solution be worthwhile?"

3. Brainstorm for a solution.

4. Evaluate the possible solutions

5. Do a "quick and dirty" analysis of the solution.

6. Use an analytic framework for a more thorough analysis.

7. Ask yourself other important questions about the business.

8. Evaluate the industry.

We'll go through each of these steps in detail here.

1. Identify a problem

We all have opinions, and we all think our opinions are worthwhile; we're not shy about sharing our opinions and ideas.

With opinions usually come gripes: people have complaints about something they own, think they know a better way to make a pizza, they moan about the lack of an iPhone app that can pay their parking meter, or complain about how difficult it is to find someone to take care of their pets when they're on vacation.

Where most people see problems, entrepreneurs see opportunities; whereas most people talk about their grievances, entrepreneurs act on these complaints, forming businesses that will make money by providing solutions to those problems.

Identifying a problem, then, is equivalent to identifying an opportunity. And since so many people have opinions and complaints about things, mining those complaints can point you in the direction of an interesting business solution.

2. Ask yourself if a solution is worthwhile

Finding a solution to a problem needs to be worthwhile on two levels: as the basis for a viable business and as something worthwhile to you personally. Whether or not something is worthwhile to you personally is a very different question than whether or not it could be a successful product or business.

There are three things that should line up if you're going to be successful and wealthy in your line of work:

1) You should do something you love.

2) You should do something you're good at.

3) There should be a market for what you're doing.

Evaluating the size and potential of a market isn't that difficult. Many people can analyze a particular market and come to a good conclusion about whether or not that market is big enough to accommodate a successful business. Points one and two, though, are things that only you can decide, based on your own abilities, interests, and values.

Passion and belief

Entrepreneurs are salespeople. They are people who have to demonstrate the value of their product or service, sometimes shamelessly pitching it to complete strangers or to people who will tell them time and again they have no interest in what they're selling.

Entrepreneurs don't just have to sell a product, though; oftentimes they have to sell the idea of a business to a bank loan officer in order to get money to buy equipment, or sell the idea to suppliers of key products who might be reluctant to supply some new, unknown, and untested company.

The key attribute of a good salesperson is passion, and passion usually comes from belief. If you really believe in the product or service you're selling, your passion will shine through to everyone you meet.

Passion is contagious. Look at Michael Scott from The Office. That guy, for all his flaws, loves the paper business and honestly believes he is doing something good for people by selling them Dunder Mifflin paper.

If you were in charge of buying office supplies for your company and some dispassionate person from a large paper or office supply company came to see you, giving you a memorized and monotone pitch about why you should buy their paper, and then Michael Scott came in to do the same sales pitch with much more exuberance, energy, and enthusiasm, you'd probably buy from Dunder Mifflin.

If you don't feel passionate about something, you're probably not going to be a good representative of it. And if you don't really believe in something, you're probably not going to feel passionate about it. If you don't feel passionate about something, it's going to be very hard to motivate yourself to keep at it, whether it's making you a lot of money or not.

When you think about a potential business, ask yourself if you really believe in that business, if you can really be passionate about it. If you think there's a need for a better paper or office supply company, you could form one to address that need. But unless you feel the type of passion for your product that Michael Scott feels for his, it's going to be very difficult for you to compete with the Michaels of the world, despite how incompetent those people might be in so many other areas.

Aptitude

Are you good at what you're thinking of getting into? If your business idea is providing math tutoring to young children in lieu of babysitting them, you really need to be good at two things: math, of course, but more importantly in communicating with young kids.

You might be a mathematical genius, but if you don't know how to talk to a nine-year-old child, you're not likely to be a very successful math tutor. You'll also need to know how to communicate with the real customer, the kid's parents, since they're the ones who will be paying you and will want to make sure you can deliver what you claim you can.

Identify the key things you need to be good at in a particular business. In business terms, these are known as "success factors." Someone thinking of opening a restaurant might think that the key success factor is being a good cook. This is not always the case.

What is the most successful restaurant in history? The answer is McDonald's. Does McDonald's make the world's best hamburger? I don't think anyone, regardless of how much they love that company, would say they make the best hamburger on the planet. Why, then, are they so successful? Maybe because they've identified and mastered other success factors for restaurants that most other food-service businesses do not look at, like standardization, site selection, and value.

McDonald's knows that offering a consistent, standard, pretty good meal at a reasonable price at a high-traffic location will generate more success than offering a fantastic meal, inconsistently prepared and delivered, at a high price in some place that people have a hard time finding. Because the food and service are consistent across the world, customers know what to expect when they go into a McDonald's, so it's harder to disappoint them.

If you were to go into a new restaurant and order a fifteen-dollar burger, you might complain that the service wasn't good or that the place forgot the pickles; you're unlikely to do that with a place you're familiar with (your expectations are already formed, and McDonald's knows how to manage to those expectations), and you're less apt to complain about a relatively inexpensive product than one that sells for a higher price.

So, the critical success factor for McDonald's might be standardization rather than food quality.

Understand what the critical success factors are in the business solution you're considering. For McDonald's the critical factor isn't just making a great hamburger, but making a great hamburger thousands of times a day, every day, no matter how busy they are, and having all the hamburgers taste the same (so that people don't get disappointed that the hamburger they're having today isn't as good as the one they ate at your place yesterday).

Ask yourself if you're really good at all of those things, or just one of them (being a great cook and being able to make a great burger).

If you've identified what it takes to succeed, are passionate about your business, and are good at delivering the critical success factors, then you're on your way to having a good business.

Conscience

Let's suppose you've identified an opportunity, a solution to a problem. The product you could deliver is something that you feel passionate about, and you're talented in the areas that are the critical success factors. What other things should you consider?

Ask yourself if the business you're thinking about is something you can feel good about. Is it something you can be proud of? Is it something that does well? Is it safe?

Simplicity

Is the business simple? Simplicity is a great thing. Look at the beauty of the iPod. When Sony, Samsung, and other companies were making fancier and more complicated products with lots of bells and whistles, Apple came along and delivered a simple-looking white rectangle that stored and played music.

It wasn't trying to be a device that controlled your television, started your car, and toasted your bagel;

it was just a small music-playing device. There's simplicity of design and simplicity of product. The iPod has both; it looks simple, and if someone asked you what it does, you wouldn't have to use a lot of fancy jargon or have an advanced engineering degree to explain it to them: "It stores and plays my music."

Simple businesses have a lot of advantages over complex ones. One area of complexity is regulation. If you're thinking of starting a business in an industry in which there are a lot of regulations, or with a lot of different government agencies that you have to answer to, you're going to have a lot more frustration and lost focus than the person who starts a business that isn't regulated.

Complexity in process is another type of problem. If you have a product that requires fifteen different stages of manufacturing, then there's a much greater chance that something can go wrong than if you just bought a finished product and sold it in one simple step.

Complexity can come in forms that aren't easily visible at first. For example, suppose your idea for a business requires a big up-front investment and ongoing large infusions of capital to keep it going.

A capital-intensive business (one that requires a lot of money to start up and operate) is financially more complex than one that's not capital intensive, if for no other reason than the capital-intensive business relies on money always being available. That's a layer of uncertainty and complexity that a business that doesn't require a lot of money to set up and operate doesn't have to deal with.

Finally, there's technological simplicity. Generally speaking, if something is more high-tech, it will be more complex to manage. There's a problem, however, with fast-changing, high-tech, and complex businesses: the chance of being blindsided is greatly increased.

For example, Warren Buffet, the greatest investor that has ever lived and one of the wealthiest businesspeople on earth, usually avoids investing in tech companies. Why? Because he says he doesn't understand them. Does that mean he's not very smart? No, Buffet likes companies like Coca-Cola and Wrigley's more than Google or Apple because, in effect, he says that in twenty years people will probably still be drinking Coke and chewing gum the way they do today; but it's not clear that they'll still be using Google's services or Apple's products in the same way, or if those companies will even exist in the future.

In a fast-changing industry like technology, a new product can emerge that will make the existing product obsolete. The iPhone might make GPS makers extinct; similarly, a new product that comes out tomorrow might make the iPhone obsolete. It's unlikely, however, that some new product will come around that will displace Starbucks, Coke, Wrigley's, Frito-Lay, or Kentucky Fried Chicken.

3. Brainstorm for a Solution

Let's say you've gotten through Steps 1 and 2: you've identified a problem, and you believe that delivering a solution to the problem could create a good business opportunity.

Not every new solution can be the basis of a good company. How can you know in advance if the idea you have is a good one, one that can become a successful business, or one that doesn't have a market?

In this section, we'll look at a number of methods for potential new businesses, doing analysis to see if a new business has a good chance of success, and identifying the critical variables that determine if a good idea equates with a good business.

Brainstorm

Brainstorming is just unedited, undirected, and unscripted thinking. It's identifying some problem, and then allowing any thought about the solution to the problem to come up and be developed. It works best in small groups or teams, but can be done on your own.

In brainstorming, any possible solution can be proposed, discussed, added upon, and mapped out. By not rejecting any idea out of hand, brainstorming allows for a large number of ideas, some conventional, some crazy, and some just very creative, to come out and be expanded upon. Here are the steps of brainstorming on a business:

- Identify the problem:

There's no grocery store in your area that sells organic produce.

- Gather a brainstorming group:

You might try to get a group of five people together to brainstorm on solutions to the problem. Typically, your brainstorming group could be you and a few friends, but if you can bring in some people who know about business in general (a local businessperson, for example) and someone who knows about the specific kind of business you're thinking about (in this case, someone who knows something about selling food), that could make the group even better.

- Brainstorm around the solution:

You would write down the problem and then invite any possible solutions, writing all of them down. You're not evaluating any idea right now, and you're not discouraging any idea. The craziest ideas sometimes lead to the most creative solutions.

4. Evaluate the possible solutions

Discuss the solutions identified in the brainstorming session. Some ideas might be eliminated, and others expanded upon. Brainstorming isn't expected to give you all the answers all the time, but it's a useful tool for drawing out different possibilities to consider when thinking about a potential new business idea.

5. Do a quick and dirty evaluation of the business

Once you've identified a problem and brainstormed on solutions, you might have an idea that you think is a good one. During your brainstorming session, you discussed setting up a roadside stand that would sell organic produce, opening a store that would sell organic foods, starting a mail-order or Internet-based business that would sell organic food, and renting booths at local street fairs to sell organic food you'd buy from a farmer in your area.

You decide to evaluate the idea of selling organic food through the Internet. You think you could get a simple web site up that would allow people to place orders for food that you could deliver once a week, on Saturday afternoons.

The farmer you'd buy from would drive a truckload of food to your place on Saturday morning, you and your friends would split up the delivery into individual bags and then deliver them to the people who had placed the orders.

You've identified a problem, brainstormed on a lot of possible solutions, and have narrowed the ideas down to one that you want to evaluate more thoroughly. What to do now?

Understanding your market

First, you need to understand who your market is. Who would buy your produce? To answer that, you probably need to know how much the vegetables would sell for. If the price, with delivery, is about the same as the vegetables in the supermarket, then you might be able to sell your organic food to everyone who buys vegetables.

You'd be selling not only produce, but convenience: for about the same price as it costs to buy veggies at the market, your customers can have fresh, local, organic produce brought to their homes.

If the price is substantially higher than the veggies at the market, though, then you are aiming for a more specialized market: people who value the convenience of delivery and are willing to pay a lot more for organic food. Who would pay more for groceries in return for not having to drive to the store every week? Perhaps busy people, the elderly, handicapped people, and people who don't have cars or access to the store.

Of course, to know what the price will be, you'll need to run some numbers. Let's assume that the farmer says that he can bring produce to your house every week for 30 percent less than the cost of produce at the local supermarket. He says he'll need a minimum order of $500 a week to make the trip worthwhile.

You estimate that it would take you and your business partners about three hours to separate all the produce into small orders, and another three hours to deliver all the food. You figure that you'll spend an additional five to six hours a week taking orders over the Internet, accounting for the money the business brings in, and doing other managerial tasks. If you pay yourself and your friends $10 an hour for a total of 12 hours of work each week, you estimate you can make $380 a month by charging the same price that the grocery store does for its produce.

Expected Number of Customers ("# of units'") each week - 50

Expected Sales per Customer ("revenue per unit") - $20

Total Expected Revenues per Week - $1,000

Expected Cost of Vegetables ("COGS") - $500

Expected Labor Costs - $120

Number of people working - 3

Number of hours/person - 4

Wage per hour - $10

Total Operating Costs - $620

Total Expected Net Profit - $380

You now have a decent idea about how your business will work, what the main cost items will be, what you'll be providing to customers (good food and convenience), and how much money you could make.

By selling vegetables at the same price that produce sells for at the supermarket, you figure you could sell to everyone who shops for produce at the market.

Let's take things to the next level, by doing two relatively simple types of analysis of the business idea.

6. Frameworks to evaluate your business idea

An analytic framework is just a structure that you can follow to evaluate something in more detail.

There are many different analytic frameworks that are used to evaluate business ideas, but two that are easy to use, common in many types of businesses, and taught in most business schools are SWOT and Porter's Five Forces analyses.

SWOT Analysis

The acronym SWOT stands for "Strengths, Weaknesses, Opportunities, and Threats." This type of analysis was developed by Albert Humphrey at Stanford University in the late 1960s, and is a simple way of thinking about different categories of a business.

The SWOT analysis is pretty self-explanatory: list your prospective business's major strengths and weaknesses, and what you think the largest opportunities your company will face, as well as the biggest threats to your company's business model.

There's not a lot of analysis that accompanies a SWOT; it's simply a framework to help you think about your business. Of course, if you have an easy time coming up with weaknesses and threats and a hard time identifying strengths and opportunities, that in itself should tell you something.

Here's what a SWOT analysis of the organic food delivery business idea might look like:

Strengths

- *Sole provider of a product with good demand*

- *Ability to sort and deliver product cheaply*

- *Very low overhead (no store, low fixed costs)*

- *Convenient (internet-based) ordering system*

Weaknesses

- *Don't have a large advertising budget*

- *People don't know who we are; don't know if they can trust us*

- *Our product line is limited to vegetables*

Opportunities

- *Could expand product line (dairy products, breads)*

- *Could expand customer base*

- *Deliver to restaurants, senior centers*

- *Could expand reach by recruiting kids from other neighborhoods for delivery*

Threats

- *Supermarket could start offering low-priced organic food*

- *Easy for other people/companies to enter our business*

- *Regulatory threat if our product isn't high-quality (makes people sick) or if established competitors complain about our operation*

Porter's Five Forces Analysis

Porter's Five Forces is named after Michael Porter, a professor at Harvard Business School who created the concept in 1979. According to Porter's method of analysis, there are five "forces" acting on any business, and you should attempt to measure "who has the power" in each of these. The five forces are: Supplier Power, Buyer Power, Threat of Substitutes, Degree of Rivalry, and Barriers to Entry.

We won't go through all of these areas in detail, but here's a brief examination of the Five Forces for your organic produce company.

1. Supplier Power

Supplier power is the power of suppliers to set prices. The other forces we'll look at influence it, but essentially it's the amount of power that suppliers of a product or service have over the buyers of those goods or services.

Your company will be the "supplier" of organic food, conveniently delivered. How much "power" do you have over the buyers of this service? Can you raise your prices regularly without losing business? Is your product so much better than the alternative (driving to the grocery store) that customers will pay more for it? The amount of supplier power you have will be dependent on many things, including the other forces we'll examine.

An example of someone with a high degree of supplier power is U2, the rock band. There is only one U2, and if you want to see them in concert, you have to pay the highest price that they and their promoters think you're willing to pay. U2's uniqueness gives them a lot of supplier power, but it's not infinite; they realize that if they price their services (the cost of seeing them) too high, you might decide to do something else (choose a substitute to seeing U2 in concert).

By contrast, the band at the bar downtown singing U2 songs can't get away with charging much for you to see them, as there are hundreds of other bands around the country that are just as good as they are (in other words, they're more of a commodity than U2).

An example of a company with a high degree of supplier power is Microsoft. If you need MS Office, you pay whatever Microsoft sets the price at. In most cases, the more "commoditized" your service or product, the less supplier power you have.

Your product is fairly unique. Organic vegetables are certainly different from standard ones, and the delivery aspect makes the product even more special. If you were just another guy at the local farmer's market standing at a table selling carrots and cabbages, you'd be just another commodity; there would be many other people there selling the same things, and the only thing that sets you apart from other sellers would be a good location or lower prices.

The less "commoditized" your product, the less you have to worry about competing just on price. Another way of saying this is, the more differentiated and unique you can make your product from competing products, the more supplier power you will have.

2. Buyer Power

This is the opposite of supplier power: it's the power of the buyer of a good or service over the supplier of that product.

Suppose there's only one organic farmer within driving distance of your house. Since he's the only supplier, he could potentially wield a lot of power over your business. If he sees that your business is doing well, he could jack up his prices and you'd have no alternative but to continue buying from him.

On the other hand, if there are many organic farmers in the area that are willing to sell and deliver to you, then the larger number of suppliers of a commoditized product (one organic potato isn't that different from another) would suggest that supplier power is low and, conversely, that buyer power might be high.

3. Threat of Substitutes

This is the ability of a user to substitute your product or service with another one. The higher the level and availability of substitutes to what you offer the less power you're likely to have as a supplier of your product or service to the market.

Substitutes aren't simply "obvious" ones. A Honda Accord is an obvious substitute for a Toyota Camry, but anything that buyers might do or choose that gives them a similar result to owning a car is a substitute. For example, riding the bus or riding a bike could be substitutes for buying a Toyota.

In the U2 example, if the price of the U2 concert ticket is $100, you might "substitute" going to the concert with buying a few U2 CDs for $40, going to a different concert for $25, or going to dinner and a movie for $50. A substitute for hiring a babysitter isn't just hiring a different sitter, but staying at home, taking the kids with you when you go out, or leaving the kids home alone (assuming they're old enough to take care of themselves).

What are the substitutes for your organic vegetable business's product? The obvious one is nonorganic vegetables: a person might decide to buy a nonorganic turnip rather than your organic one. Less obvious substitutes might be frozen vegetables, meats or grains (if the price of vegetables rises a lot, people might cut back on them and use more chicken, bread, or fruit instead of veggies), growing their own food (starting a garden at home), or eating out.

4. Degree of Rivalry

This is basically a way of asking, "how intense is the competition?" Gas stations have a high degree of rivalry; they advertise their prices on big signs every day, are all over the place, sell a commoditized product, and have to do everything possible (offer car washes, run in-house convenience stores, etc.) to get you to choose their company over any of the others. There is intense competition in that sector, just as there is in the restaurant business, lawn care business, and many other areas.

For your business, the most obvious rival would be markets that sell vegetables and, in particular, organic vegetables. If there are many supermarkets in your area, we can assume that there's a high degree of rivalry. The businesses would all advertise heavily, offer specials that would lure people into buy certain things (and pick up some vegetables while they're at the store), know what its competitors are charging, and be able to switch its prices quickly in response to you or anyone else offering similar produce at more competitive prices.

5. Barriers to Entry

This is a way of thinking about how easy or difficult it is for other people or firms to enter your business area.

Are the barriers to entry for your business high or low? Considering that there are no special licenses to sell your product, no specialized expertise, no major start-up or operating costs, that you don't yet have a "brand" or reputation that will keep people coming to you even if the local supermarket starts selling organic vegetables, and that the "switching costs" are low (it doesn't cost a customer anything to stop buying from you and start buying from someone else), it would appear that the barriers to entry for the business you're considering are very low. In other words, just about anyone can enter this business and compete with you, so the "entry barriers" are low.

Porter's and SWOT are by no means the only ways to think about and evaluate your business idea, but they're good places to start. They're easy to remember and apply, and they force you to consider many of the elements of your business that you might otherwise gloss over or forget to include.

Now that we've gone through the very casual (brainstorming) and more formal (SWOT and Porter's) ways of thinking about your potential business, we should consider a number of other things that every new entrepreneur should ask themselves about the business they're thinking of starting.

Other important questions about the business

What are you providing?

This may sound like a stupid question, but it's important to think beyond the specific product or service your business is offering. You must understand what needs you are providing. This will help you identify why people might want your product, and what potential substitutes they have for it.

What does Starbucks provide? Most people would say "coffee", but if you really think about it, you'll see that they provide much more than that. Howard Schulz, Starbucks's CEO, believes that his company provides a "third place": a place outside of the home and the office that is inviting, comfortable, dependable, and familiar.

For many people, the cost of a coffee is the "rent" they pay to relax on Starbucks's real estate: the cost of having chairs and tables for an hour to meet with friends or the cost of having a couch to relax in.

Starbucks also provides routine, and routine is comfort; stopping by Starbucks every morning on the way to work or school is part of a daily ritual for millions of people, as much a part of their morning routine as brushing their teeth.

When you think of it this way, the competition for Starbucks might not necessarily be Tully's or McDonald's but a park, community center, or any other place that people might choose to meet at instead of Starbucks.

The organic vegetable business is actually providing many things. It's providing vegetables, certainly, but it's also providing convenience (delivery), health, and peace of mind (many people will buy because they believe that organic foods are healthier or less harmful to the environment than inorganic foods are).

Are the customers always right?

The idea that the customers are always right is a mistaken one. In blind taste tests, Pepsi scores higher than Coke, a fact that led Coke to change its formula and offer "New Coke" many years ago - a decision that's viewed as one of the greatest business mistakes of all time.

You can see why Coke executives would have been worried: "People are telling us they like Pepsi more than Coke! We have to change the taste!" The problem was that people weren't actually saying that: people vote with their pocketbooks, and Coke consistently outsells Pepsi. The fact is that people are married to the Coke brand. Even if a competing product tastes better, people won't switch from the brand they love. Besides, how many people drink soda blindfolded anyway?

You could argue that the customer was right in this case - they did like the taste of Pepsi more - and that it was the company that was wrong in thinking that just because the customer liked the taste of Pepsi more they would switch.

Customers aren't very good at being right about things they want that are big departures from what's already available. What does this mean? Before the iPod came out, most people were listening to music on portable CD or tape players.

Sony may have asked a number of customers what they wanted in a portable music player, and the customer, not being able to envision something radically different from the CD player they were used to carrying around may have said "a smaller CD player" or "a CD that holds a lot more music."

Sony went that route, promoting "evolutionary" products like "mini discs" and others that have faded into obscurity. Apple, on the other hand, created something entirely different. The customer (and Sony) viewed their product as "CD players" and tried to make a better one; Apple viewed the product as portable music and decided that they didn't have to deliver that music on CDs or tapes, but on a small hard drive. The iPod was born, and the rest is history.

For revolutionary (as opposed to evolutionary) change, customers often have no idea what they want. If you ask someone who travels a lot what they want, they might tell you something that's just a minor evolution of an existing product or service: "I want bigger seats in the airplane and shorter lines at the airport." You're not likely to hear someone say something revolutionary like, "I want to be able to teleport, making airlines and airports obsolete." That's an extreme example, of course, but you can get a sense of why the customer is usually more "right" when they're thinking of incremental change to existing products, or when, in the case of New Coke, factors such as "brand" and "loyalty" weren't factored in.

Is there a market for the product?

It's a common mistake to assume that just because you think something is a good idea that others will buy into it also. The best way to answer this question is to do some basic market research.

You don't have to be an expert in marketing to do good basic market research. For your vegetable business you could call a few supermarkets that sell organic produce and ask them if there's demand for the product (or visit the store and see if shoppers are considering the organic options they have there); you could contact your local markets and ask why they don't carry more organic foods (maybe they used to), but there was no demand for the product); you could do surveys (ask 100 shoppers if they have ever bought organic, why or why not, and if they would consider buying organic if the price were the same as nonorganic and the food were delivered to them).

Here are some questions and suggestions for starting your market research:

1. Identify a company that is likely to be your competitor. Research the company and the product it has that yours would compete with. Make a list of the strengths and weaknesses of that company and its product, and a similar list of your company and product (even if your company and product are still just in your head right now).

2. Who buys the product your competitor produces? Why? What type of person is most likely to buy the competitor's product, and what type is most likely to buy yours?

3. Find some users of the competitor's product and find out what they like and don't like about the product. Would they recommend the product to a friend? Why or why not? It's very hard to take a customer away from a company they're satisfied with: would your success depend on taking away its customers, or would you be appealing to a group of customers that your competitor hasn't addressed?

4. Have other companies tried to compete with the leader in the field and failed? Why? How could you be successful when they failed?

5. How big is the market for your product, and what are the trends of the market? For example, the market for food catering might be over $1 billion nationally, but only about $250,000 in your town. The trend might be from ethnic foods to healthy, locally grown foods.

What's your competitive advantage?

This is an extremely important question. If you can't answer it, you may want to rethink the business you're in.

A business's competitive advantage is the reason that they're able to succeed when others fail, why people will want to use their product or service rather than a competitor's.

There are many, many possible sources of competitive advantage: A business can be the cheapest provider of something, offer the highest-quality product, the fastest service, the most-convenient location, the most trustworthy brand, the smallest product or the largest. The competitive advantage also might not rely on the product or service the business offers; the competitive advantage could come from being the first to market, having the best management or the most money, or any number of other things.

A competitive advantage does not have to be real; they can simply be perceived. A successful lawn care business might not be the best or cheapest, but if people in the neighborhood see their friends using the company, they might assume that it's the best option and sign on as a customer.

Whatever business you're in or thinking of getting into, you should be able to identify and easily explain what your competitive advantages are or will be.

What price should you charge?

There are lots of ways to approach this question: you could set your prices based on what a competitor is charging, (i.e., if you run a gym, you might charge slightly less than the gym down the road, or you might believe you can charge more because you offer things that they don't.); you could make your financial models and set your prices at a level that will give you the profit you need to stay in business; you can do market research to estimate how much your market would be willing to pay for what you're going to sell.

Whatever you decide to base your price on, you have to be able to explain and justify it to customers, lenders, investors, and others. The more data you've collected and analyzed, and the more evidence that supports your price, the more persuasive the argument will be that people are willing to pay what you're asking.

Is the business scalable?

This isn't an important topic if you don't ever expect to grow beyond a certain, smaller size, but it becomes relevant if you have ambitions to expand and become a large company one day.

Scalability is the ability of a company to grow efficiently. Some businesses are very scalable, and others aren't. An example of a highly-scalable business is Microsoft, which creates computer operating systems, puts those systems on discs, and then sells the software either online as a downloadable product, or physically, through the mail or at stores.

Microsoft can produce one million units of its product almost as easily as it can produce 100. Making an additional unit, or an additional million, just requires having more blank discs, downloading the original file more times, and putting more products in the mail.

What's an example of a business that isn't very scalable? Something that depends on the talents of an individual, whose skills and abilities can't be recreated easily. The world's best barber, for instance, can only cut so much hair. If he can't train other people to be fantastic barbers, then the amount of money he can make in his business is limited by how many people walk into his shop each day. Furthermore, if he's sick or on vacation, the business shuts down, and he can never expand by opening a second, third, or fourth shop.

A lot of internet-based businesses, by contrast, are very scalable, as their owners don't have to do a lot of additional work to accommodate additional viewers or customers.

Is the business sustainable? Are there good long-term prospects for the business?

We looked at how high-tech products carry a risk of being blindsided and rendered obsolete through the emergence of new technology, but even some simple businesses can burn brightly, briefly, and then burn out.

Sustainability isn't determined just by the "trendiness" of a product, though. Increasingly, the term is used to describe environmentally friendly products. A product that can be recycled is more sustainable than one that is used and thrown away. Similarly, sustainability can be based on economics: if the solar industry can't survive without massive government subsidies, then is it really a sustainable one?

What are the major risks?

An entrepreneur isn't someone who just takes advantages of opportunities; it's someone who is aware of the risks their business faces before, during, and after launch. In fact, more time should be spent working on minimizing risks than on maximizing opportunities: good things can take care of themselves; it's the bad things that will suck the time and energy away from you if you don't plan adequately.

Many people focus so much on the upside potential of their business idea, getting so carried away with the dream of success that they fail to consider the downside risks. When you actually launch your business, it's possible you'll be so busy "putting out small fires" (paying bills, collecting money owed by customers, dealing with employees or suppliers, handling insurance or regulatory issues, and doing the other small but necessary tasks to stay alive) that you won't be able to calmly evaluate business risks and how to minimize them.

It's not a lot of fun to think of all the things that could happen that could hurt or even kill your business, but isn't it much better to do this exercise before you launch a business than to find out afterward that something has gone wrong and you could lose everything because you failed to plan (in some cases not just your business, but your personal assets, your credit, your reputation, and more)?

Brainstorm every possible problem that could arise. Identify the ones that carry the greatest risk (either have the greatest chance of occurring or would do the most harm if they did occur) and try to find ways to minimize or eliminate those risks.

For example, with your organic vegetable business, what would happen if your farmer and sole supplier shut down the farm (lost it to the bank, retired, sold it, or just decided to stop growing organic food)? What would happen if someone got very ill from eating some of the food you provided and sued you and your company? What if the large grocery store down the street started offering cheap organic food? What happens if one of your delivery drivers hits someone while making a delivery? What happens if someone finds out that the food you're selling as organic really isn't organic (maybe the farmer was putting in regular produce with his organic product)?

Who could you find that is an expert on business and on business risk? Who can offer you some guidance, advice, and protection from your risks? The person or company that you buy insurance from would be a good place to start; insurance people are in the business of assessing risk and "pricing it out." They can offer you insurance to protect you from many types of negative events. Maybe you should set up a meeting with an insurance agent and get their opinion of your business risks and ways to lower them. There might even be some insurance products to protect you from certain risks.

Lawyers and tax consultants can help. You might be able to find and download useful contracts to use with suppliers (e.g., "if you fail to deliver your produce on time, you'll pay a penalty of $X" or "you promise that all the foods supplied will be certified organic unless otherwise stated"). It's not a great idea to skimp on legal and tax services, but if you shop around you can usually find good deals or at least cheap temporary solutions that will tide you over until you can direct more money to them.

If you don't understand the risks of your business, you don't really understand the business. If you don't create strategies and use tools to minimize risk, all your "opportunity planning" could get flushed down the toilet.

Evaluating your industry

It's not enough to evaluate your own company; you must evaluate the industry in which you will operate. The Porter's Five Forces analysis is a great way to start the examination of your industry. Let's build on that analysis by looking at a few important questions. You should ask these questions and be able to come up with the answers about the industry you're considering becoming a part of.

The value of luck and timing

Never discount the value of good luck. A very large number of successful people achieved their success more from luck than from hard work, intelligence, or commitment.

During the Internet bubble that burst in 2000-2001, you could have been a student with no business experience whatsoever, written a business plan in Crayola on a piece of toilet paper, and found people to give you millions of dollars to launch any business that had the name "dot com" in it.

Successfully launching the business had much more to do with the timing and type of business than it did on the abilities of management, the quality of the product, or any other factor.

Conversely, if you're trying to come to market with a new GPS device for automobiles, you're fighting an uphill battle: iPhone and other mobile devices are making stand-alone GPS devices obsolete. You could have the best dashboard-mounted GPS system ever seen, but you'd be fighting for a piece of a quickly shrinking pie.

Luck is one of the most important factors and gets the least amount of respect. You might get lucky and bring a product to market at just the right time; more often, though, you'll need to rely on your wits and work to get you to the top.

Many years ago, Burger King touted its "flame broiled" process of making hamburgers, which it believed created a product that was much better than McDonald's traditional grilling.

There was a major change in the industry, though, when customers started buying breakfasts at hamburger chains: McDonald's was able to make eggs, sausages, pancakes, and other food on the same grills it used to make hamburgers, while Burger King had to totally revamp its kitchens, spending a ton of money on new equipment, employee training, and additional space. The "fast food breakfast rush" was a monumental change that was simply a lucky break for McDonald's and an unlucky one for Burger King.

Sometimes, your business gets a lucky break that propels it to success. It's just as possible, though, for the luck to fall your competitor's way, leaving you out in the cold. You can't plan for luck, but as Samuel Goldwyn said, "The harder I work, the luckier I get."

Industry size and growth

No business exists in a vacuum. Every company has suppliers, customers, competitors, and dynamics that need to be analyzed if you're going to compete successfully in the industry you're in.

You've already looked at one method of analyzing your company vis-a-vis the industry it's in: Porter's Five Forces Analysis. In this section, we'll look at some things you would like to see in an industry that will put the wind in your business's sails rather than its face.

Industry characteristics that can be good for your company

One venture capitalist puts it this way: "There are only three things I want to know: Is the industry large? Is the industry growing? And what share of the industry can your company get?"

If you're launching a business in a large and fast-growing industry, you'll have a much greater chance of success than if you launch in a small and shrinking one. The players in a dying industry fight fiercely for the last remaining scraps of business; you don't want to get caught in the middle of a price war with companies that have a lot more money than you do, and could act irrationally.

Being in a large growth industry is great, but for it to translate into real success, you'll have to become a significant player. The share of a market you own, unsurprisingly known as your "market share," is important, but so is the share of the market to the total industry. For example, you might believe you could get sixty percent of the market for your product, but if the product is only two percent of the industry, that might not be as attractive as getting twenty percent of a product that makes up thirty percent of the industry.

Confused? Look at it this way. Say you want to be a music producer and you're going to find and produce hip-hop albums. Sounds good - hip-hop is a big market and is growing; it's also a big portion of the overall music industry.

There are a lot of hip-hop producers out there, but you figure you have a great niche: you're going to focus on Christian hip-hop artists. This might not be a bad idea at all. Christian music has a strong following and other products (books, movies, TV shows) aimed at that segment of the market have been successful.

If you can make a case that the Christian hip-hop market is large, getting larger, and that you can take a big share of the industry because there aren't a lot of producers focusing on this area, you could have a great business.

On the other hand, if you wanted to produce country-western/hip-hop crossover albums - hip-hop albums for country-western fans - you might be able to take a huge share of that market, but it would be such a small segment of the hip-hop industry that it probably wouldn't be very successful.

Competition

Sometimes, you should worry more about the lack of competitors than by the presence of them. You might think it's great that no one else is offering organic produce in your town, that it means the field is clear for takeoff and that you'll be the only, or at least the first, supplier. But the absence of competitors could also mean that there's no market for what you're planning to offer.

Some basic market research should help clarify if there's a real opportunity that others simply haven't identified, or if the absence of competition comes with a good reason.

Management

Having a good management team is very important, but that in itself is usually not enough to overcome the challenges of being in a bad business.

To quote Warren Buffett: "When a great manager meets a bad business, it's usually the reputation of the business that survives." Only a few superstar managers can turn the tide of a company that is in decline. For example, Jerry Yang, of Yahoo, thought that he could restore his company's position as the leader in search engines; this prompted him to reject a generous offer from Microsoft to buy the company, and, eventually, to his getting fired by his board of directors.

Even a poor manager can run a great business, but a great manager rarely succeeds with a poor company.

4. How to Avoid the Pitfalls of Starting a Business

Common mistakes and misconceptions of new entrepreneurs:

1. Focusing solely on invention and ignoring innovation

2. Not asking why your product or service doesn't already exist.

3. Being too optimistic about your budget

4. Expecting other people to make the business a success

5. Focusing on too narrow a customer group

6. Getting into heavy labor or capital-intensive businesses

7. Coming up with far-fetched businesses

1. Focusing solely on invention and ignoring innovation

Entrepreneurs and inventors are two very different groups of people, but many people tend to believe that if they don't invent some new product or service, they can't be successful entrepreneurs. That's far from the truth.

Rollin King and Herb Kelleher didn't invent the airplane or any part that goes in it, but they did create one of the most efficient and profitable airlines in the world, Southwest. King and Kelleher's genius lay in changing the business model of airlines, streamlining costs, and focusing on the customer (that may not sound revolutionary, but many of the "big name" airlines treat their customers almost as annoyances).

Similarly, Michael Dell didn't invent the personal computer, but he created an approach to building and selling PCs that customers loved, and Dell has built the company into one of the most successful companies in the world.

Craig Newmark didn't really invent anything when he started Craigslist, but he changed the way that classified ads, once the domain of print newspapers, could be posted and viewed.

The message should be obvious: you don't have to invent something new to make a great business. Identifying and filling a need can lead to great success.

A related myth is that your product has to be a fantastic, revolutionary one in order for the business to be successful. You don't have to start with a grandiose idea. Rather than launching a business that will try to take on Amazon or eBay, why not start with one that tries to be the best in a narrower field, or launching in an area that isn't served by someone else (what Craigslist, LinkedIn, and Wikipedia all did)?

2. *Not asking why your product or service doesn't already exist*

Some good ideas are truly unique. Others might not be unique, but you can make them a success by getting them to market quickly, offering great service, or otherwise differentiating your product from others out there. However, some good ideas have been tried and tested and failed.

3. *Being too optimistic about your budget*

A budget is composed of inflows (revenue from sales) and outflows (money spent on setting up and running the business). Most entrepreneurs make two budget mistakes, the effects of which compound and create real problems for the company. First, they overestimate their revenues (remember earlier, when we talked about tempering your optimism and setting targets that were easy to hit or surpass at first?). Second, they underestimate their costs.

My advice in regard to estimating costs is the mirror image of the advice regarding revenues: make low estimates about how much money your firm will take in, and high estimates about how much you'll spend.

In essence, you'll be making a worst-case scenario for your business. If you can stand the results of that scenario - that is, if you and your business can endure under those bad circumstances - then you're in a good position; chances are your company will do better than your worst-case scenario assumes.

Overestimate your costs and underestimate your revenues. You'll be doing the opposite of what most entrepreneurs do, and saving yourself a lot of heartache and stress by doing so.

One final thing: go out and investigate what real costs are. If you want to rent an office, don't assume you can get one for five hundred dollars just because that seems like a reasonable price to pay; go and find out exactly what an office would cost (rent, deposit, improvements, and other costs).

4. Expecting other people to make the business a success

There are two types of new entrepreneurs: those that intend to build the business themselves (or with people they have on board already) and those that expect to bring others into the business in the future. The problem with this second group of would-be entrepreneurs is that they tend to overestimate their own importance and the ease with which they can recruit others.

There are several entrepreneurs who create business ideas in which the critical success factor is in the hands of someone else, usually some professional engineer that they hope to find, somewhere and somehow, without thinking of things from that person's view. For example, the following interaction is more common than you might think:

Entrepreneur: My idea is to make a chip that you can put on children that will allow you to track them with your cell phone, so if a child is abducted; it would be easy for someone to find them.

XYZ: That sounds like a great idea for a product. What experience do you have with chips like this?

Entrepreneur: Well, I don't have any, but I'll hire someone that will make the chip.

XYZ: Okay. Let's assume that there is someone out there who can do that. Why wouldn't he or she do it on his or her own, or with someone else? Why would a person like that - probably a very high-

paid and senior engineer - decide to create a chip for your company?

Entrepreneur: *Because I had the idea.*

If you don't have the resources to build the business yourself, or with people that are already committed to the company, don't assume you're going to find someone that's going to:

1) Be able to do what you need them to

2) Be willing to work for a person less experienced than they are.

Ideas are cheap. Create a business, make some money, build a reputation, learn and grow, and raise some real money. You'll then be in a position to approach some senior star engineer at Cisco or Intel and perhaps get them to jump ship and join you on your quest.

5. Focusing on too narrow a customer group

Your customers might not be the people you expect them to be, or even people at all. No, I'm not talking about businesses aimed at pets (thought that might be the best market for your company) - your target market might be other companies, government organizations, non-profit organizations or other countries.

If you're thinking of starting a company that will turn VHS tapes to DVDs, rather than hope to find individuals that will be your customers you could approach your local library or school system. If your company sells sunglasses, perhaps you should try selling to a local skateboarding shop or sporting goods store, a place that would buy your glasses by the case, rather than to kids at school, who'll buy only one pair at a time.

Don't assume that the best customer for your product is a person like you; it might be someone, or something, very different.

6. Getting into very labor- or capital-intensive businesses

If you want to grow the business, it means hiring someone else. Keep in mind that bringing on an employee means doing payroll, adding a lot of tax work, paying social security and other costs for the employee, and a host of other work for you. Scaling up by adding people isn't a very efficient way to grow your business.

Use your mind rather than your muscle or time. Be a manager rather than an employee or laborer. Try to set up a business that can grow to ten times its initial size without requiring ten times the capital or labor needs.

7. *Coming up with far-fetched businesses*

A final mistake people make is coming up with far-fetched business ideas. Try to identify a business that you could set up and run in realistic time frames while requiring no more money than what you have available right now.

5. The Importance of your Skills

Wanting to run a business is just the first step in deciding whether you have the personality to give it a try. You must have the characteristics that will serve you well in business - desire to succeed, leadership skills, being comfortable with risk-taking, and the ability to tackle hard work.

Here's a list of other words that are often used to describe the entrepreneurial type. See how many of these words are used to describe you:

- Confident

- Determined

- Disciplined

- Innovative

- Optimistic

- Positive

You may not have all these traits, but don't let that stop you. You can pick up some of this stuff as you go along. For example, if you've never been a manager or supervisor, how can you know whether you have leadership ability? Obviously, you can't.

But by assuming a leadership role you may be surprised to learn how well it suits you. Or maybe you've taken a leadership role outside of the business world - heading up the PTA or running a community fund drive – and didn't even know it.

There is also a chicken and egg part of this emotional inventory. Starting off you may not feel disciplined, for example, but the challenge of making your weekly quota of business forces discipline on you. Most of these traits are like muscles; the more you use them, the stronger they become.

Maybe taking risks gets your knees knocking and your heart pounding. Again, as you begin to run your business and learn to take setbacks in stride, your tolerance for risks may rise.

And even if you're sure you'll never be a great communicator, you can always choose a business that plays down public contact. You don't have to go for selling a product where razzle-dazzle presentations are the order of the day; you may be able to perform a service - such as bookkeeping or medical transcription - out of the limelight, in the privacy of your kitchen.

Your skills

If you think your current job has you wearing a lot of hats, be prepared to open a hat superstore when you start your own business. First, you have to have the technical skill for your particular business (for example, computer knowledge to run a computer-based business or artistic ability to run an interior design business).

But whatever business you run, you also need many other skills. You need to become an entrepreneur. You need to be able to market your business, whether it's a service or a product. You need to be able to juggle finances - raising capital to start up and grow, managing cash flow, and purchasing. You need to work well with others - hiring employees or subcontractors, working with professional advisors, and keeping customers happy.

Your experience

You may know more than you think you know. What kind of experience do you have? Whatever business experience you have may prove helpful in starting your own business. And the more experience you have, the better off you are.

Have you ever run a business before? Even if you've always worked for a weekly paycheck, you may still have enough business experience to be successful. By simply working for a business, you may have picked up valuable information on how to run a business (or, as many disgruntled employees claim, how not to run a business).

And even if you lack business experience of any kind, if you've run a household, budgeted to buy a new car, or coached Little League, you've already picked up some important business skills in the areas of budgeting, purchasing, and personnel.

Even if you have general business experience, what do you know about the particular business you're considering? Have you ever worked in the field before?

Obviously, the more you know about the field, the better off you'll be. But even if you've never been near someone who has done this kind of work, you may be able to translate your experience in a related area into valuable help for your business.

For example, you have experience in a retail clothing store. Now you want to start your own mail-order business to sell clothes you design. You don't have experience in mail order, but you might be able to use your knowledge of selling clothes to research fashion markets and create a catalog. You know clothes; you know selling. Don't sell your experience in any other business short.

Your financial picture

Your personal financial picture, rosy or not, will affect how you view your business - how much you can afford to put into it and what you expect to get out of it.

For example, if you're retired and living on a pension, then a small business may only have to supplement your income. The same is true if you have a full-time job and only expect the business to be a sideline for generating extra cash. But if you've been laid off, your business may just be your bread and butter.

The kind of business you choose is influenced a lot by your bank book. How much do you have to invest? How much can you borrow? Some businesses require a small endowment to get started. It may cost thousands of dollars to buy the equipment or inventory needed to get up and running.

Are you in a financial position to come up with the bucks you need to get going? Many other businesses such as day care services, cleaning services, and even consulting businesses - can be started with a few hundred dollars.

6. Getting Prepared

Once you've determined that a small business is something you want and will be good at, you have to narrow down the field to find the business that's perfect for you. Here's where your creativity and ingenuity pay off.

Fine-tune your idea

You know you want to start a business. Great! You may even know what type of business you want to run - a consulting business, selling products through catalogs, online, or whatever. But these vague ideas have to be fine-tuned before you can proceed. You have to work out all the particulars. So let's get specific.

You can't simply decide to be a consultant or start a catalog or online business. You have to clearly define the service you'll be offering as a consultant or the products you'll be selling through a catalog or online.

If you plan to be a consultant, presumably you know the general area you'll be consulting in (for example, management advice or computers). But you have to get even more specific.

For example, as a consultant for computers, will you be providing advice to individuals or to corporations? Will you write a newsletter or blog about computers or service them door-to-door?

This might seem like a simple exercise, but give it a whirl: to help you focus your idea, try explaining it to others in 30 to 60 seconds. You might see that in your first few explanations you're about as clear as mud. Try to be specific. Try to address the four Ws: what, who, where, and when.

- What will you be doing? What product or service will you be offering? Why would anyone pay good money for this? Can you actually make money doing this (after factoring in your costs and time)?

- Who will you be selling your product or service to once you run out of friends and relatives? The guy on the street? Fortune 500 companies?

- Where will you be selling your product or service? Are you going to bring every Tom, Dick, and Jane into your home for the sale? Will you put an ad in the paper? Will you sell through the Internet? Via mail order?

- When will you be selling your product or service? Are you starting part time? Full time? Are your sales seasonal?

The more concise your answers, the better off you'll be. As soon as you can describe your business concept in one or two sentences, then you have a place to begin.

Test your concept

After you think you've clarified your idea, make sure it will fly. Take the time to investigate the marketplace and find out whether there's room for you. It could take months to complete this phase of preparation for your business. But the time you take to do the legwork is time well spent.

After all, why put the money and the effort into something that has no chance to succeed? Find out at the beginning whether your concept is a winner.

Is your idea for a business practical? It may sound great as a concept, but when you get into some of the specifics - looking at cost, how you'll reach the marketplace, and other considerations - does the business really make sense?

Your business idea has to be one that's doable. You have to be able to have a realistic expectation of making a profit - if not immediately, then sometime in the foreseeable future.

For example, initially you may be buying supplies and inventory for your business at a loss or a very thin profit margin to build the business.

Think long term. Wal-Mart mandates steep annual price reductions from its suppliers. Even though you're the smallest of businesses, you should try to do the same.

Look at what economies of scale you can use to make your business more profitable. Use the Internet to shop around until you find the deal that will give you the highest profit margin.

You may be surprised to find that buying products or services (such as virtual assistants, etc.) from the other side of the planet may make your business much more profitable. Don't be afraid to go multinational right from the get-go.

Finding your niche

Suppose you conclude that your idea is just dandy. That's great. But now you have to go one step further and continue to refine your business concept so that you can find your niche.

Perhaps somewhere in your home you have a niche - a little cutout recess in the wall that's set apart from the rest of the area. That's sort of what a business niche is: it's what sets you apart from everyone else in your area.

How do you plan to distinguish yourself from the competition? Are you going to offer lower prices? Are you going to offer better service? Whatever you can do to separate yourself from your competitors will work to your advantage.

Don't think that specializing, which trims your market size, is necessarily bad. There may be plenty of room for your specialization, and it might just help you target your potential customers much more accurately.

To help you define your niche, you must size up the competition. What are they doing right? What could you do better? What's the competition failing to do that you may be able to do?

For example, suppose you want to start a residential cleaning service. Call the competition and see how they respond. Did they get back to you promptly? Were they friendly? Helpful? Were they responsive to your needs?

Their negatives can be your positives. Try out their service in your own home (even if you don't learn much, at least you'll get the windows cleaned). Were you satisfied with their work? Did you like their price?

Where the competition failed to measure up to your expectations, you can design your business to shine. You may find that they're very good. In that case, you may have to specialize (offering only carpet and rug cleaning rather than general cleaning services or offering 24-hour scheduling).

Positioning your prices

Think about the last time you made a major purchase, say a car, a dining room set, or a TV. The price tag was important, but that wasn't all you considered. If it was, you wouldn't have had to spend three hours making your decision: you'd have just asked for the cheapest one right off the bat.

Pricing won't be the only thing that separates you from your competition either, but there's no doubt it's important. Most consumers today are price conscious. The price for your goods or services must be realistic; you have to be able to make a profit from what you sell. And the public must understand your pricing policy.

If you charge lower prices than the competition, you don't want to come off as offering inferior goods or services. The public can become suspicious and worry that it's not getting quality merchandise. You may even have to explain why you charge lower prices. For example, if you can buy more economically than your competitor (because you have some special connection with a distributor), tell the public "we pass our savings on to you."

If you charge higher prices, make sure the public understands what additional benefit they're getting. Many people are willing to pay higher prices for something if there is added value, such as a personal service, a longer warranty, or a money-back guarantee.

Put your idea in writing

The best way to formulate your business concept is to put it in writing. This means writing a business plan.

A lot of folks start a small business as a casual sideline. This is a mistake. If you fail to take the business seriously, others may not take you seriously. Writing a business plan shows serious intent. There are several other important reasons to write a business plan:

- Organize your ideas. You may think you have things straight, but until you put them in writing you can't be sure. For example, you may have come up with an idea on how you'll sell your services, but maybe you didn't think about how much money you'll need to meet your advertising budget. To complete your report, you may even have to do additional research on your idea.

- Learn the strengths and weaknesses of your business concept. As you develop your plan, you'll find what aspects of your concept are real winners. You'll also learn where your idea just doesn't hold water. In the plan, you'll be addressing all aspects of business operations - personnel, marketing, and finance.

  By having the plan in writing, you'll find out what areas are strong and what areas need improvement. You may also discover that you just can't do it all by yourself. You may have to hire a clerk, hire an assistant, subcontractor, or bring in a partner.

- Have a road map for the future. Having an idea will only bring you so far. You have to be able to put that idea into action. How will you take your idea and turn it into a working business?

  What will you do first? What will you do next? A business plan can serve as your road map to bring you from point A to point B. The business plan will not only serve to get you started, it can also help you grow your business in the first few years.

- Have a presentation package to raise money. Banks and just about anyone else who's thinking about lending you money or investing in your business will want to see that you know your business. They want to see that the business is well planned and presented all together in a professional and businesslike way.

7. Miscellaneous Tips

Congratulations! You've made it through the planning phase and are now ready to officially launch your business. By taking the time to do the planning that was detailed in the previous chapters, you've done more than most entrepreneurs already, and have greatly increased your chances of success.

Here are some additional tips for you.

Finding service providers

Most people who start small companies don't have the budget to bring in a lot of expert help for things like accounting and bookkeeping, legal services, tax preparation, and other areas. If you start off small, you should be able to navigate tax and legal codes on your own, and can handle your own bookkeeping and accounting just by being organized and using a computer program like QuickBooks.

Even if you have some money that could go toward professional services, it's a good idea to at least try to do some of these things on your own. For one thing, professional fees are usually very high. Plus, you'll get a lot of good experience by putting some time into learning the basics of managing your own books, doing your own taxes, and researching legal and other issues on your own.

When you do need outside help, look online at sites that help give small businesspeople free advice. You can also check agencies for help. Look at your network of friends, relatives, and associates. It's said that there are no more than six degrees of separation between you and anyone else in the world; you might not know an attorney who would give you some good free advice, but your parents, neighbor, teacher, or a local business owner you know might.

After you've tried to handle things yourself, done some investigation for answers online, and picked the brains of people you know that have some expertise on the subject matter, you might have no other choice than to go to a professional and get some help.

Most professionals will give you an initial free consultation to hear about your business needs, and will let you know if they can help you or not, and explain how much you can expect to pay for their services.

Don't be shy about asking questions; you're the customer, and they're the person looking for another client. Ask them if they have the time to handle the job you've described, if they have experience with the type of job you're asking about, and what their best estimate of the cost.

You can check these people out on sites like Yelp or LinkedIn. If they seem honest and you feel they could be a good long-term advisor for you and your business, then go ahead and hire them. A good professional can cost a lot, but can save you a lot more by making sure things are being done the way (for example, that you're getting all the tax deductions you're entitled to, and paying the taxes you need to).

Securing other things necessary to the business

Each business has its own unique needs. Some businesses are purely "virtual," with no office space, people working online from various locations, and no special equipment or inventory necessary to keep the company functioning.

An example of this type of business might be a web site design company whose founders work from home, creating web sites and interacting with clients through emails and Skype.

Even a virtual business like the one described above needs some "procurement planning," though.

For example, the two founders, who work together on web site design, might need to have dedicated high-speed Internet connections put into their home offices.

They might need newer and more powerful computers to do their jobs more effectively, dedicated business phone lines for customers to call, and some new design software that would make their product more competitive.

For a business like a coffee shop, the list of necessary items can be lengthy: you need to lease a retail site, buy special commercial-grade equipment, maybe lease a commercial dishwasher, order uniforms, set up contracts with companies that will deliver fresh pastries to your shop every morning, buy food and beverage inventories and special cleaning materials, get approval by the fire marshal, perhaps get training in food handling, and a host of other things.

I'll assume that you've had some experience in the type of business you're planning to start (most people who open their own coffee shops have spent a lot of time working in other coffee shops and know how to operate the business), or that you can scale up your business gradually (i.e., start a lawn-care company with just your truck, a lawnmower, and a few pieces of other equipment, and then add things as the business grows).

If you're thinking about starting a business that you haven't had a lot of experience in already, especially if that business will require a lot of start-up capital, you should make it a point to speak to a few businesspeople that have experience in the type of business you want to open.

You might think that a person running a bagel shop downtown wouldn't want to speak with someone who might open a competing bagel shop on the other end of town, and you might be right.

For a business that requires inventory and equipment, there's a delicate balance between having too much and too little. You don't want to spend $10,000 on equipment only to find out that you only needed half of the things you bought; similarly, you wouldn't want to be stuck turning customers away at noon because your restaurant didn't stock enough meat or bread to make the sandwiches you're selling. Market research can help you get this balance right, but speaking with some experienced businesspeople can be invaluable in helping you get off on the right foot.

Blast off

Once you've done your planning and gone through the mechanics of setting up your company and getting any equipment, supplies, and help you need to run it, then there's nothing left but to launch.

A launch can be a big event, such as the grand opening of a restaurant, or something that is low-key or entirely inconspicuous. In any case, you're now officially a business owner and entrepreneur.

Congratulations! The things you've learned to this point, and the things you'll learn over the course of running your business - whether it's a success or failure - will be a form of education and experience that will be useful to you in just about anything you do with your life.

You have created something from nothing. You've identified a problem and have acted boldly to present a solution for it. Even if you fail, you've acted; that's what an entrepreneur does, and that's what makes them special.

Conclusion

Starting a business is an adventure. It can be scary, stressful, and painful, but it can also be extremely rewarding on many different levels.

Just about anyone can start a business. You don't need a lot of money; you don't need to be a financial or computer genius. Don't let the idea of starting a business intimidate you.

While nearly anyone can start a business, not everyone can succeed. Being successful requires a good idea, thorough planning, adequate resources, hard work, good execution, and luck. Too many entrepreneurs think that a good idea alone will be enough, but that's rarely the case; planning is an area that's often neglected, but which can give your company an edge over others.

Starting up and running a business will give you a higher quality education in all aspects of business—management, marketing, finance, accounting, human resources, strategy, operations, and more—than just about any endeavor. Running a business will teach you about yourself, forge character, and create capabilities that will be assets to you for the rest of your life. In that respect, there is no failure for the entrepreneur that plans and prepares properly; the only failure is the experience that doesn't teach you valuable lessons.

Entrepreneurship isn't for everyone, but if you believe it's the right path for you, plan wisely, and good luck with your venture.

www.ingramcontent.com/pod-product-compliance
Lightning Source LLC
Chambersburg PA
CBHW070837180526
45168CB00002B/859